A World of Food

CHINA

Clare Hibbert

CLARA HOUSE BOOKS

Minneapolis

First published in 2010 by Clara House Books, an imprint of The Oliver Press, Inc.

Copyright © 2010 Arcturus Publishing Limited

Clara House Books
5707 West 36th Street
Minneapolis, MN 55416
USA

Produced by Arcturus Publishing Limited

The right of Clare Hibbert to be identified as the author of this work has been asserted by her in accordance with the Copyright, Designs and Patents Act 1988.

Series concept: Alex Woolf
Editor: Alex Woolf
Designer: Jane Hawkins
Map illustrator: Stefan Chabluk
Picture researcher: Alex Woolf

Picture Credits
Art Archive: 7 (Golestan Palace, Tehran/Gianni Dagli Orti).
Clare Hibbert: 17 *jiaozi mixture in bowl*, 19 *egg with cracked shell*, 19 *eggs in mixture*, 19 *eggs peeled, cut and served*, 21 *mashing beans*, 21 *rice and bean mix on bamboo leaf*, 21 *zongzi on plate*.
Corbis: 4 (Michael S Yamashita), 6 (Asian Art & Archaeology, Inc), 8 (Tiziana and Gianni Baldizzone), 10 (Ron Watts), 11 (Keren Su), 13 (Gideon Mendel), 14 (Zhang Xiao Ming/Redlink), 15 (Reinhard Krause/Reuters), 16 (Keren Su), 18 (Michael S Yamashita), 20 (So Hing-Keung), 22 (Earl & Nazima Kowall), 23 (Earl & Nazima Kowall), 24 (Dean Conger), 25 (David Turnley), 26 (Wolfgang Kaehler), 27 (Michael S Yamashita), 28 (Liu Liqun), 29 (Gail Mooney).
Photoshot: cover (Imagebroker.net).
Shutterstock: 5 *chopsticks* (Evlakhov Valeriy), 9 (Xuanlu Wang), 12 (Emmanuel R Lacoste), 17 *Chinese cabbage* (Elena Schweitzer), 17 *minced pork* (Jacek Chabraszewski), 17 *green onions* (ultimathule), 17 *ginger* (Norman Chan), 17 *jiaozi* (Andrea Skjold), 19 *cinnamon and anise* (omkar.a.v), 21 *three zongzi parcels* (Feng Yu).

Cover picture: A market scene in Beijing, China.

Every attempt has been made to clear copyright. Should there be any inadvertent omission, please apply to the publisher for rectification.

Library of Congress Cataloging-in-Publication Data

Hibbert, Clare, 1970-
China / Clare Hibbert.
     p. cm. -- (A world of food)
Includes bibliographical references and index.
ISBN 978-1-934545-09-6
1. Food habits--China--Juvenile literature. 2. Cookery, Chinese--Juvenile literature. 3. China--Social life and customs--Juvenile literature. I. Title. II. Series.

GT2853.C6H53 2010
641.300951--dc22

3 1559 00216 3168

2009038013

Dewey Decimal Classification Number: 394.1'2'0951

ISBN 978-1-934545-09-6

Printed in China

www.oliverpress.com

Contents

China and its Food

China is home to more than a quarter of the world's people. Food is so important there that people often greet each other with the words *Chi le fan mei you?*, which literally translate as "Have you eaten yet?"

China is named after its first emperor, Qin. From around 221 BCE, Qin brought together a number of different lands in eastern Asia. Today, China is the third-largest country in the world, covering about a fifth of the continent of Asia. Its main language, Mandarin Chinese, has more than 880 million speakers, far more than any other language. With its growing population and booming economy, China is on the way to becoming a superpower.

▲ Three generations eat dinner together at home in the suburbs of southern China.

World-class cuisine

Food is central to life and culture in China. The Chinese believe that good health comes through eating well. The history of cooking in China goes back a long way. The style of cooking was established by the late 14th century, when the Ming dynasty of emperors came to power. Today, Chinese cuisine is thought of as one of the world's finest

4

because of its amazing array of ingredients, cooking methods, and flavors.

A typical Chinese meal has rice or noodles served with several small dishes to share. These contain bite-sized morsels of vegetables, seafood, or meat. The perfect Chinese meal offers a variety of textures, tastes, and different kinds of cooking.

▼ This map shows China's key cities and regions.

CHOPSTICKS

In China, people do not used a knife and fork to eat their food. Instead they use a pair of tapered sticks called chopsticks. The sticks are held in the right hand, between the thumb and fingers, and are used like pincers to pick up pieces of food. They are usually made of bamboo, wood, or plastic, but more expensive ones are made from metal, jade, or ivory.

History of Food

China is one of the world's oldest civilizations. Its first farming villages appeared around 7000 BCE. People grew rice and millet. Later, they cultivated wheat, which they used to make the first noodles.

By 4500 BCE, people were using steamers for cooking. They made wine by fermenting millet or rice. Tea was grown from around 1000 BCE. By 400 BCE, most people cooked food in bite-sized pieces to save fuel (it cooked faster). As a result, knives were no longer needed and chopsticks became the main eating utensil.

Silks and spices

The Silk Road was established by the first century BCE. It was not one road but a collection of trade routes. It brought spices and other new foods into China from India, Persia, and the west.

Braising was introduced by the Mongols when they took over China in the late 13th century. Cooking meat slowly in a pot over the fire was part of their nomadic heritage.

▼ Shaped like an elephant, this beautiful carved jade wine vessel was made when the Shang emperors ruled China (1500–1050 BCE).

Modern times

Chinese cooking styles did not really change after the 14th century. In the 20th century, China became a communist republic. The push to modernize led to terrible hardship and food was scarce. The Great Famine (1958–61) claimed at least 15 million lives.

For a long time, certain foods were not available, but by the turn of the 21st century, China's leaders were more relaxed. There was greater freedom to import foreign foods, opening up a new world of ingredients to the people of China.

▶ A painting on a vase shows workers drying tea leaves. The vase dates to the days of the Ming emperors (1368–1644).

TEA IN CHINA

Tea drinking began in China and tea is still the country's most important beverage. It is drunk after meals and during special tea ceremonies. Tea shops are important places to meet with friends. Various loose teas are popular, including green tea, black tea, wulong tea, and jasmine-scented tea. The Chinese also prepare tea that has been compressed into solid bricks.

Climate and Soil

Due to its vast size, China has a greatly varied climate. This affects what foods naturally grow in different regions, what crops can be raised, and what dishes people eat.

Most of China's landscape is mountainous. Tibet, in the southwest of China, has mostly alpine pasture, with a short growing season of only 90 to 120 days. It is cold almost all year round. The north-west and far north of China have dry grasslands and deserts, including the bleak Gobi Desert, which has bitterly cold winters. Even in the capital, Beijing, night-time temperatures in the winter drop to −4°F (−20°C).

River valleys

China also has areas of forest (mostly in the north-east and southwest), natural and sown meadows for raising livestock, and mudflats. Only about 15 percent of its land can be cultivated. Most of this lies in the

▼ The valley of the Yangtze (or Yellow) River is a patchwork of farmers' fields.

SEASONAL WINDS

Monsoon winds influence China's climate. From November to April, cold, dry monsoons blow in across the plateau of Siberia and Mongolia, giving northern China its cold, dry winters. From May to October, warm, wet summer monsoon winds blow in from the Indian Ocean and the western Pacific, bringing about 80 percent of China's total yearly rainfall.

valleys of the three great rivers that cross eastern China – the Huang He, the Yangtze, and the Xi Jiang.

The most northerly river, the Huang He, has a flood plain of especially rich, black soil. This region is generally dry and cool and the principal crops are wheat, millet, and corn. The Yangtze flows through central China. This region has long, humid summers, lasting from April to October, and cold winters.

Southern China, which includes the valley of the Xi Jiang, is wet and warm. The climate here is subtropical and tropical, with trees staying green all year round. Rice, tea, and exotic fruits can be grown in the south.

▼ Boats at Guilin on the River Yulong in Guangxi, southern China. The climate here is warm and rainy.

Farming

There are about 200 million farmers in China. They grow a range of cereal crops, vegetables, and fruits. They also keep livestock and raise fish, such as carp, in ponds.

Onions, cabbages, radishes and other hardy plants are cultivated all over the country. Other crops require the particular conditions of the warm, wet south or the cooler, drier north.

▲ These stepped fields or terraces of rice, called paddies, grow in the southern Chinese province of Guangxi.

Regional crops

Rice, grown in the south, is China's most important crop. Other crops on southern farms include water lilies (for their tuberous lotus roots), peanuts, bamboo (for its young shoots), and sweet potatoes. Fruits include citrus, lychees, and bananas.

In the north, the main cereals are wheat, millet, and corn. Vegetables include turnips, potatoes, and soybeans. The main cultivated fruits are apples, pears, peaches, apricots, and jujubes (or Chinese dates). Jujubes are used in traditional Chinese medicine.

Farm animals

Pigs are the main food animals. Around 60 percent of all the meat eaten in China is pork. Poultry accounts for 18 percent and beef for just 9 percent. Farmers keep chickens and ducks partly for their meat but mostly for their eggs.

Many farmers keep water buffaloes, horses, mules, or donkeys as beasts of burden. The average farm is just 1.5 acres, so it often makes sense to have a working animal rather than a tractor – it costs less to buy, is cheaper to "run," doesn't break down, and may even provide milk.

▼ A water buffalo pulls a plow for a farmer in southern China. This flooded field is being prepared for sowing rice.

GROWING RICE

China produces more rice than any other country. Farming rice is very labor-intensive. Workers hand plant the seedlings and must keep the flooded fields, called paddies, free of weeds. The plants are harvested by hand with sickles or with mechanical harvesters. It is hard work separating the grains from the stalk and husk by hand. Sometimes the job is done by animals trampling on the stems or with threshing machines.

Food and Culture

The Chinese usually eat three meals a day. Most meals are eaten in the home, but workplaces provide food, and eating out in restaurants is growing more popular.

In rural areas, some women still cook all the meals, even if they also work in the fields. However, in most Chinese families the cooking is shared between adults and older children. Where different generations live under the same roof or even just nearby, grandparents may prepare the evening meal.

For many Chinese, lunch is the main meal of the day, eaten at their work canteen or bought from a street vendor. Eating out (once reserved for special occasions because of the cost) is becoming more common, including eating dim sum.

DIM SUM

Dim sum is a special brunch made up of lots of light dishes, served with tea. Favorite items include steamed dumplings; steamed buns; rice noodle rolls; bean, turnip, or lotus-root cakes; chicken feet in black-bean sauce; and *congee* (rice porridge). Some restaurants prepare as many as 60 dishes. Diners order plain rice and noodles from the kitchen, but select smaller dishes from trays or trolleys brought around by waiters.

▶ Vendors, like these in Beijing, sell a range of delicious fast foods.

Table manners

The Chinese usually eat at a round table. All meals, even breakfast, are made up of many dishes. The diners each have their own bowl of rice, then help themselves to the shared dishes. These include a range of tastes – salty, sweet, sour, hot, and bitter. They have usually been cooked in a variety of ways – for example, steamed, braised, boiled, stir-fried, and roasted.

Elderly people are offered food first. People do not spear food or poke around in the shared dishes. It is also rude to leave chopsticks sticking out of rice or to point them at anyone. Burping is perfectly acceptable, though – it expresses appreciation of the food!

▲ Factory workers in the Chinese capital, Beijing, enjoy a lunch that includes northern fried and steamed breads.

Confucianism, Taoism, and Buddhism are the three main belief systems in China. Although Confucianism and Taoism are not really religions, their traditions affect people's morals and lifestyles in a similar way to religious teachings.

Confucianism, Taoism, and Buddhism have certain shared ideas. They are all concerned with finding balance and they all place more emphasis on human behavior and relationships than on gods.

Rituals and rules

Confucianism is based on the teachings of the thinker Confucius, who lived around 500 BCE. Confucius thought that rituals were very important. Confucian writings include guides for how balanced meals should taste and rules for how to act at the table.

Taoism

Taoism brings together many ancient Chinese folk beliefs and traditions. It underpins Chinese medicine and its followers believe that certain foods can cure illnesses or give good health.

An important Taoist idea is yin yang. Yin represents female, black, night, water, and earth. Yang is associated with male, white,

▶ A Taoist monk prepares tea at the Qingyang Temple in Chengdu, Sichuan province.

day, fire, and air. These opposites depend on each other for harmony. The yin-yang principle influences Chinese food. A balanced menu has contrasting flavors, textures, temperatures, and colors.

Zen Buddhism

Buddhists believe in reincarnation – being reborn after death in a new body, which may be that of an animal or another human. Many Buddhists do not eat meat, including followers of Zen Buddhism, which came to China in 520. Buddhist chefs are responsible for Chinese cuisine's range of tofu-based and other vegetarian dishes.

THE CHINESE YEAR

Many Chinese festivals are associated with special foods. These festivals follow a lunar calendar, based on the Moon's orbit around the Earth, rather than Earth's movement around the Sun. However, a 12-month lunar year is only 354 days long. Just as the solar calendar adds an extra day every leap year to stay linked to the seasons, the Chinese add an extra month (called an intercalary month) seven times every 19 years.

▼ Young Tibetan Buddhist monks carry away blessed food during their Great Prayer Festival.

New Year

New Year is the most important festival in the Chinese year. It is a time when families come together and, of course, food plays a big part in the celebrations.

▲ Dancers prepare to perform the lion dance, as part of the New Year celebrations.

New Year begins on the first day of the first lunar month and the festivities last for two weeks. People clean their homes, settle old debts, and buy new clothes. They let off fireworks and enjoy parades, such as the dragon and lion dances.

New Year's Eve banquet

The celebrations begin with a wonderful feast. The foods bring good fortune in the coming year. The spring rolls resemble gold bricks, while vegetables and dumplings are made to look like coins. Steamed clams symbolize being open to good fortune. Tangerines, oranges, and kumquats are also all thought to bring luck.

New Year gifts

People give each other money at New Year, sometimes in red envelopes because the color is believed to scare away evil spirits. They also take gifts of lucky oranges, sweets, and chocolates when they visit friends and relatives.

RECIPE: New Year dumplings (jiaozi)

Equipment
- colander • bowl • baking sheet
- teaspoon • saucepan

Ingredients (for 20 dumplings)
- ¼ small head Chinese cabbage, finely chopped • ¼ teaspoon salt
- ¼ cup (65g) minced pork
- 2 large green onions, chopped
- 1 garlic clove, crushed
- 1½ teaspoons soy sauce
- 1½ teaspoons toasted sesame oil
- ¼ tablespoon rice wine
- 1½ teaspoons fresh ginger, finely chopped
- 1½ teaspoons corn flour
- 20 round dumpling (gyoza) skins

1 Place the cabbage in a colander with the salt for 30 minutes, then squeeze out the water.

2 With your hands, mix the cabbage with the pork, green onions, garlic, soy sauce, sesame oil, rice wine, and ginger in a bowl.

3 Dust the baking sheet with corn flour. Place a teaspoonful of dumpling mixture in the middle of a dumpling skin, wet the edges, then fold to make a half moon, pinching the edges between your thumb and forefinger. Place on the baking sheet. Repeat to make 20 dumplings.

4 Cook them in boiling water for five minutes, then drain.

5 Serve with a dipping sauce made from ¼ cup (50ml) of soy sauce and 1½ tablespoons (25ml) of water.

Qing Ming

The spring festival of Qing Ming is held to honor the dead. It is celebrated together with the Cold Foods Festival, which falls the day before.

Jie Zitui

During the Cold Foods Festival, no fires are supposed to be lit, so traditionally everyone eats only cold foods – for example, cold rice porridge. According to one story, Cold Foods honors Jie Zitui. His friend, the duke, offended him. To drive Jie Zitui from his forest hiding place, the duke's men lit a fire, and Jie Zitui burned to death. Deeply sorry, the duke ordered that no fires should be lit in memory of the proud Jie Zitui.

Tomb tidying

At Qing Ming, people visit the graves of their ancestors. They sweep them clean, pull up any weeds, light incense, and leave offerings. These might include whole, cooked chickens, roast ducks, hard-boiled eggs, fruit, tea, and wine.

▶ At Qing Ming, relatives place offerings on their family graves and light incense sticks.

After the tomb ceremony, the family shares a delicious picnic of tea eggs, egg tarts, steamed spring rolls, and pancakes called *popia*, which may be filled with seafood and vegetables.

RECIPE: tea eggs

Equipment
- saucepan • sieve • knife

Ingredients (serves four) • 4 large eggs
- ¼ cup (50ml) soy sauce • 3 tea bags
- 2 ½ tablespoons (35ml) rice wine • ½ tbsp. sugar
- ½ star anise, crushed • ½ cinnamon stick

1 Place eggs in a saucepan of cold water and bring to the boil. Reduce heat and simmer for ten minutes. Run cold water over eggs, then drain.

2 Lightly tap each egg, then roll on a hard surface to crack shell. Do not peel.

3 Add soy sauce, tea, rice wine, sugar, and spices to 1¾ cups (400ml) of water and bring to the boil. Simmer uncovered for 20 minutes.

4 Add eggs and simmer for a further 30 minutes. Turn off heat and leave eggs to cool in the mixture.

5 Peel the egg shells and cut eggs into quarters. Strain the cooled cooking liquid and spoon some onto the eggs.

Dragon Boat Festival

The Dragon Boat Festival marks the arrival of summer. People race boats in honor of Qu Yuan, a statesman and poet who lived around 300 BCE.

▲ Dragon boat racing to honor Qu Yuan is a colorful activity.

According to legend, the king became angry with Qu Yuan, so he jumped into the Miluo River to avoid exile. People took to the water to save him, but failed. Then they threw in little parcels of sticky rice, called *zongzi*, to stop the river dragon from eating him.

Racing boats

People mark the festival by going to watch long, narrow dragon boats race on rivers and lakes. As part of the celebrations, people eat *zongzi*. Some contain savory pork and chestnuts, while others have sweet fillings. Traditionally, people dabbed their faces with wine to ward off evil. Today they drink the wine instead.

All kinds of cakes

In earlier times, the nobility gave each other cakes made from apricots, mulberries, and water chestnuts or even rose petals to mark the festival. Sometimes the cakes were made to look like centipedes, lizards, scorpions, snakes, or toads, in the hope that the recipient could avoid that poisonous creature.

RECIPE: zongzi

Equipment
- saucepan • masher or handheld mixer
- wooden spoon • sieve • two bowls
- measuring spoons • steamer

Ingredients (for 10 [or 5] *zongzi*)
- 15-ounce (425g) can adzuki beans
- ½ cup (85g) sugar • ¼ cup (55g) unsalted butter
- ½ tablespoon vanilla extract • ¾ cup (150g) glutinous rice
- 20 dried bamboo leaves, or 5 sheets of frozen banana leaf, defrosted, approx. 8 x 8 inches (20 x 20cm)
- 10 (or 5) x 6-inch (15-cm) pieces of string

1 Cook beans in boiling water for one minute, then drain.

2 Return beans to pan and roughly mash, then stir over a low heat for two minutes.

3 Add sugar, butter, and vanilla. Use handheld mixer to turn mixture into a smooth paste. Cook for 20 minutes over low heat until very thick. Leave to cool.

4 Rinse rice in cold water until water runs clear. Soak in cold water for two hours, then drain. If using bamboo leaves, soak the leaves in cold water for 20 minutes, then drain.

5 Use two bamboo leaves to make a cone-shaped parcel. Put two teaspoonfuls of rice at the bottom, then a spoonful of bean mixture, then cover with more rice. Fold over the leaves and secure with string. Repeat to make 10 parcels. For banana leaves, use a single sheet and fold it over four times as if wrapping a present.

6 Steam parcels over boiling water for 30 minutes. Serve immediately.

Moon Festival

Moon cakes are one of the most delicious celebratory foods that the Chinese eat. People bake or buy them to mark the autumn full moon, or Moon Festival.

▲ Hong Kong Chinese light paper lanterns to celebrate the autumn Moon Festival.

The Moon Festival falls on the 15th day of the eighth lunar month. Originally it was a kind of harvest festival. People gave each other gifts of fruit and cakes shaped like the full moon. They left offerings of melons and other fruits outside in their gardens to honor the moon goddess, Chang E. In Chinese folklore, her husband, an archer called Yi, shot down nine different suns and saved the world from burning.

Jade Rabbit

People also left yellow beans for the moon rabbit, known as Jade Rabbit. The Chinese say that the markings on the Moon's surface show a rabbit using a mortar and pestle. He is thought to be pounding up gold, jade, and jewels to make the elixir of immortality – a liquid that gives a drinker everlasting life.

Since the Moon is thought of as feminine, the Moon Festival is an extra-special time for women and girls. They clean the house from top to bottom, decorate the walls with colorful posters, bow to the full moon, and light incense for Chang E.

People also enjoy round moon cakes, filled with a sugary paste of fruit, nuts, seeds, or beans. Some cakes are very elaborate, as the dough lid that forms the top of the cake is usually stamped with a meaningful design.

REBEL CAKES!

In the 14th century, the Mongol rulers of China ordered an increase in taxes. Chinese rebels hid small pieces of paper inside their harvest-festival moon cakes, giving details of when and where to meet to start the rebellion. The strategy worked, and the Mongols were thrown out of China in 1368.

▶ A baker finishes off some moon cakes. The cakes can be sweet or savory – these have a delicious duck-egg filling.

Regional Cooking

Everywhere in China, cooks use three basic flavorings – soy sauce, rice wine, and ginger. What's added to these, and the kind of dishes cooks prepare, depends on the region.

Most Chinese are Han people, with other ethnic groups making up less than nine percent of the population. Han cooking is what is traditionally considered Chinese food. It has four regional styles.

North and south

Northern cooking involves a variety of techniques – braising, baking, deep-frying, stir-frying, grilling, and stewing. Noodle dishes are flavored with soybean paste, garlic, and sesame oil. Peking duck is the region's most famous dish, and people also enjoy steamed buns and nut dishes.

▼ Peking duck is a northern speciality. The birds are soaked in water, hung, glazed with syrup, and then slowly roasted until they are brown and shiny.

Southern, or Cantonese, food is known for its seafood and non-native ingredients, such as peanuts, peppers, and sweet corn. Flavorings include garlic, fermented black beans, and oyster sauce. Roast suckling pig, bird's nest soup, braised chicken liver with sliced snake and abalone with fish and pork balls are all favorite dishes.

East and west

Eastern cuisine mixes sweet, sour, salty, and savory tastes – often within one dish! Pork is a popular meat, served up as pork with dragon well tea (pork stir-fried with a kind of green tea), spareribs with sweet-and-sour sauce, pork kidney in sesame sauce, white-cut pork, and ham with honey syrup.

Western Chinese food is hot, sour, and salty. Before chillies arrived in the 16th century, the heat came from brown Sichuan pepper. Typical western dishes include hot and sour soup, kung pao chicken, "ants climbing trees" (minced pork with thin, see-through noodles known as glass noodles) and spiced beef.

▲ Customers at a fish market in Hong Kong, China.

FOOD FROM THE SEA

Seafood is popular all over China, but especially in coastal areas. Inland, farmed river or pond fish are eaten. The Chinese favor firm, white-fleshed sea fish, such as grouper and sea bass, rather than oily tuna or salmon. Other seafoods include shark fins, prawns, snails, abalone, and crab. The Chinese also harvest sea cucumbers, which they dry, and jellyfish, which are preserved by salting.

Ethnic Foods

Apart from Han Chinese, there are people from more than 50 other ethnic groups in China, all with their own cooking styles and traditions.

▲ In Yunnan province, southern China, a Dai market seller prepares rice noodles wrapped in bamboo leaves.

The Bai people live mostly in Yunnan and number just under two million. Their staple food is rice, which they eat pilaf-style – browned in oil and then simmered in stock.

Other southern peoples

The Dai people, also from Yunnan, cook their rice in hollowed-out bamboo tubes. Bamboo yields bamboo worms, too – a favorite Dai snack. The Dai make a fermented vegetable dish using sour papaya sauce and sun-dried vegetables.

The Miao, most of whom live in Guizhou, also like sour foods. They make sour soup from fermented rice or tofu water and use it to braise poultry, fish, or vegetables.

The Dong, who live in Guizhou, Hunan, and Guangxi, make a dish called oil tea. This is a broth of rice, tea oil, tea leaves, and peanuts, to which they add shallots, spinach, fried rice, peanuts, pig's liver, and offal.

CHINESE FOOD TERMS

Word	Pronunciation	Meaning
chao fan	chow fun	fried rice
chao mian	chow mein	fried noodles
dian xin	tien SING	dim sum
dou fu	tofu	bean curd
guo	gwaw	wok
hao you	how yu	oyster sauce
kao ya	kow YA	roast duck
kuai zi	KWAI tze	chopsticks
jiang you	JIANG yu	soy sauce
jiao zi	djow tze	dumplings

Western peoples

Nearly 5.5 million Tibetans live in China, in the far southwest. Their diet is based on barley, which is roasted to make *tsampa*. Tibetans also eat spicy stews of yak, goat, or mutton. They use tea leaves, yak butter, and salt to make a filling drink called yak-butter tea.

The Uyghur of the far northwest number nearly nine million people. They often start their meals with soup and dumplings. The sauce for *langman*, a popular Uyghur noodle dish, changes with the seasons. Uyghurs also like to eat spit-roasted meat accompanied by flatbreads.

▶ A woman pours yak-butter tea into a pot. This rich, creamy drink helps keep out the cold on the plateaus of Tibet.

27

Global Influences

China's trade with other civilizations over its long history brought in new foods, which became part of the country's cuisine. At the same time, many Chinese have taken their style of cooking to other parts of the world, especially since the 19th century.

▲ People harvest chili peppers on Hainan, an island off southern China. Chilies were introduced to China from Central America.

Wheat, barley, and beef were among the first imported foods to China. They arrived several thousand years ago from western and southern Asia. Later, Silk Road merchants imported new ingredients, including saffron and other spices.

Modern imports

From the 16th century, foods from the Americas appeared, including mangoes, peppers, chilies, and tomatoes. Around the same time, explorers brought back delicacies such as shark's fins and bird's nests from southern Asia.

Since the 1990s, many Western food outlets have appeared in China. Global brands such as McDonalds are especially popular among the young.

Chinese food abroad

Since the 19th century, millions of Chinese have left their homeland and made new lives elsewhere, particularly in the Americas, Australia,

South Africa, and Southeast Asia. Immigrants who opened restaurants adapted their dishes to suit local tastes and ingredients. Chop suey and fortune cookies were both invented in the United States, for example.

What Westerners call Chinese food is less complex than the real thing. Westerners are put off by delicacies such as chicken feet and offal, so these do not even appear on the menu. Western restaurants offer far more beef and other meat dishes than are eaten in China, and serve fewer vegetables. Fewer cooking techniques are used, too, with most dishes either stir-fried or deep-fried.

MSG

Monosodium glutamate, better known as MSG, is a seasoning used by chefs in Chinese restaurants, especially abroad. It was first produced in its pure form in the early 20th century in Japan and it is not part of traditional Chinese cuisine. The seasoning is used for its intense salty flavor.

▼ Chinatown in New York City contains one of the world's largest overseas Chinese communities.

Glossary

abalone A type of edible sea snail.

BCE Stands for "Before the Common Era," the years before the birth of Jesus.

bird's nest soup Soup that is made by poaching cave swifts' nests in stock.

braised Cooked gently, usually in stock.

Buddhism A religion based on the teachings of the Buddha. Buddhists believe that enlightenment can be reached by suppressing worldly desires.

communist A system in which the government controls the production of goods and the running of services.

Confucianism A belief system in which rituals and good behavior are practiced to create an ordered society.

dim sum A buffet meal made up of many small taster dishes.

dragon boat A narrow boat with a prow carved into the shape of a dragon's head.

famine A time when food is scarce and many people die of starvation.

fermenting Allowing a food to be broken down, for example by yeast.

flood plain The low-lying land in a river valley that is prone to flooding.

incense A resin that gives off a sweet smell when burned.

ivory A hard, creamy-white material that makes up the tusks of elephants.

jade A hard, green precious stone.

Mandarin Chinese The main language of northern and southwestern China.

monsoon The seasonal shift in wind direction that causes wet and dry seasons in Asia.

mortar and pestle A bowl (mortar) and stick (pestle) used to pound substances.

nomadic Describes the wandering lifestyle of animal herders.

offal The entrails and organs of a butchered animal.

oyster sauce A rich sauce made from boiled oysters and seasonings.

paddy A flooded field for growing rice.

pilaf-style Cooking method where grain is browned in oil and then braised.

republic A nation governed in the name of the people and ruled by a president.

soy sauce Sauce of fermented soybeans.

staple A food that forms the basis of the diet of the people of a particular country or region.

Taoism A belief system in which people try to live a balanced life in order to understand the central life force.

threshing Separating grain from husk.

tofu Soft food rich in protein made from mashed soybeans.

tuberous Describes thick, fleshy roots.

Further Information

Books

Festivals and Foods of China by Jianwei Wang (Mason Crest, 2006)

Festive Foods! China by Sylvie Goulding (Chelsea Clubhouse, 2008)

Food Around the World: China by Polly Goodman (Wayland, 2006)

Moonbeams, Dumplings and Dragon Boats by Nina Simonds, Leslie Swartz and The Children's Museum, Boston (Harcourt, Inc, 2002)

Taste of Culture: Foods of China by Barbara Sheen (KidHaven Press, 2006)

World of Recipes: China by Julie McCulloch (Heinemann, 2009)

Websites

china.mrdonn.org/food.html
All about ancient Chinese foods and food customs

www.circletimekids.com/WorldLibrary/countries/China/
Contains simple recipes for Chinese dishes that children can make.

www.historyforkids.org/learn/china/food/
Contains information about ancient Chinese food.

www.kiddyhouse.com/CNY/
Contains resources on the Chinese New Year, including traditional foods.

DVDs

Cooking with Kids: Exploring Chinese Food, Culture and Language (Ni Hao Productions, 2009)

Families of China (Master Communications, Inc, 1999)

Index

Page numbers in **bold** refer to pictures.